D0174702

A Little Spoonful of

Chicken Soup for the Teenage Soul™

No-Hair
Day

If you are turning 16, you stand in front of the mirror scrutinizing every inch of your face. You agonize that your nose is too big and you're getting another pimple—on top of which you are feeling dumb, your hair isn't blonde, and that boy in your English class has not noticed you yet.

Alison never had those problems. Two years ago,

she was a beautiful, popular and smart eleventh-grader, not to mention a varsity lacrosse goalie and an ocean lifeguard. With her tall, slender body, pool-blue eyes and thick blonde hair, she looked more like a swimsuit model than a high school student. But during that summer, something changed.

After a day of lifeguarding, Alison couldn't wait to get home, rinse the saltwater out of her hair and comb through the tangles. She flipped her sun-bleached mane forward. "Ali," her mother cried, "what did you do?" She discovered a bare patch of skin on the top of her daughter's scalp. "Did you shave it? Could someone else have done it while you were sleeping?" Quickly, they solved the mystery—Alison must have wrapped the elastic band too tightly around her pony tail. The incident was soon forgotten.

Three months later, another bald spot was found, then another. Soon Alison's scalp was dotted with peculiar quarter-sized bare patches.

After diagnoses of "it's just stress" with remedies of topical ointments, a specialist began to administer injections of

cortisone, 50 to each spot,
every two weeks. To mask her
scalp, bloody from the shots,
Alison was granted permission
to wear a baseball hat to school,
normally a violation of the strict
uniform code. Little strands of
hair would push through the
scabs, only to fall out two weeks
later. She was suffering from a
condition of hair loss known as
alopecia, and nothing would

stop it.

Alison's sunny spirit and supportive friends kept her going, but there were some low points. Like the time when her little sister came into her bedroom with a towel wrapped around her head to have her hair combed. When her mother untwisted the towel, Alison watched the tousled thick hair bounce around her sister's shoulders. Gripping all of her limp hair between two fingers, she burst into tears. It was the first time she had cried since the whole experience began.

As time went on a bandanna replaced the hat, which could no longer conceal her balding scalp. With only a handful of wispy strands left, the time had come to buy a wig. Instead of trying to resurrect her once-long blonde hair, pretending nothing had been lost, Alison opted for a shoulder-length auburn one. Why not? People cut and dyed their hair all the time. With her new look, Alison's confidence strengthened. Even when the wig flew off from an open window of her friend's car, they all shared in the humor.

But as the summer approached, Alison worried. If she couldn't wear a wig in the water, how could she lifeguard again? "Why—did you forget how to swim?" her father asked. She got the message.

After wearing an uncomfortable bathing cap for only one day, she mustered the courage to go completely bald. Despite the stares and occasional comments from less-than-polite beachcombers—"Why do you crazy punk kids shave your heads?"—Alison adjusted to her new look.

She arrived back at school that fall with no hair, no eyebrows, no eyelashes, and with her wig tucked away somewhere in the back of her closet. As she had always planned, she would run for school president, changing her campaign speech only slightly. Presenting a slide show on famous bald leaders from Gandhi to Mr. Clean, Alison had the students and faculty rolling in the aisles.

In her first speech as the elected president, Alison addressed her condition, quite comfortable answering questions. Dressed in a T-shirt

with the words "Bad Hair Day"
printed across the front, she
pointed to her shirt and said,
"When most of you wake up in
the morning and don't like how
you look, you may put on this
T-shirt." Putting on another T-shirt
over the other, she continued.
"When I wake up in the morning,
I put on this one." It read,
"No-Hair Day." Everybody

cheered and applauded. And Alison, beautiful, popular and smart—not to mention varsity goalie, ocean lifeguard and now, school president with the pool-blue eyes—smiled back from the podium.

— *Jennifer Rosenfeld and Alison Lambert*
   Chicken Soup for the Teenage Soul

The Home Run

On June 18th, I went to my little brother's baseball game as I always did. Cory was 12 years old at the time and had been playing baseball for a couple of years. When I saw that he was warming up to be next at bat, I decided to head over to the dugout to give him a few pointers. But when I got there, I simply said, "I love you."

In return, he asked, "Does this mean you want me to hit a home run?"

I smiled and said, "Do your best."

As he walked up to the plate, there was a certain aura about him. He looked so confident and so sure about what he was going to do. One swing was all he took and, wouldn't you know, he hit his first home run! He ran around those bases with such pride—his eyes sparkled and his face was lit up. But what touched my heart the most was when he walked back over to the dugout. He looked over at me with the biggest smile I've ever seen and said, "I love you too, Ter."

I don't remember if his team won or lost that game. On

that special summer day in June,
it simply didn't matter.

— *Terri Vandermark*
  Chicken Soup for the Teenage Soul

The human spirit
cannot be paralyzed.

If you are breathing
you can dream.

MIKE BROWN

After a While

After a while you learn the
        subtle difference between
        holding a hand and
        chaining a soul,
And you learn that love
        doesn't mean leaning
        and company doesn't
        mean security,
And you begin to accept your
        defeats with your head
        up and your eyes open,
        with the grace of an adult,

not the grief of a child,
And you learn to build all your
roads on today
because tomorrow's
ground is too uncertain
for plans.
After a while you learn that
even sunshine burns if
you get too much.
So plant your own garden
and decorate your

own soul, instead
of waiting for
someone to bring
you flowers.
And you learn that you really
can endure...
That you really are strong,
And you really do have worth.

— *Veronica A. Shoffstall, written at age 19*
Chicken Soup for the Teenage Soul

My First
Kiss, and
Then Some

I was a very shy teenager, and so was my first boyfriend. We were high school sophomores in a small town. We had been dating for about six months.

A lot of sweaty hand-holding, actually watching movies, and talking about nothing in particular. We often came close to kissing—we both knew that we wanted to be kissed—but

neither of us had the courage
to make the first move.

Finally, while sitting
on my living room couch, he
decided to go for it. We talked
about the weather (really),
then he leaned forward. I put
a pillow up to my face to
block him!

He kissed the pillow.

I wanted to be kissed
sooooooo badly, but I was too

nervous to let him get close. So
I moved away, down the couch.
He moved closer. We talked
about the movie (who cared!),
he leaned forward again. I
blocked him again.

I moved to the end of the
couch. He followed, we talked.
He leaned...I stood up! (I must
have had a spasm in my legs.) I
walked over near the front door
and stood there, leaning against

the wall with my arms crossed, and said impatiently, "Well, are you going to kiss me or not?"

"Yes," he said. So I stood tall, closed my eyes tight, puckered my lips and faced upwards. I waited...and waited. (Why wasn't he kissing me?) I opened my eyes; he was coming right at me. I smiled.

HE KISSED MY TEETH!

I could have died.

He left.

I wondered if he had told anyone about my clumsy behavior. Since I was so extremely and painfully shy, I practically hid for the next two years, causing me to never have another date all through high school. As a matter of fact, when I walked down the hallway at school, if I saw him or any other great guy walking toward me, I quickly stepped into the nearest room until he passed. And these were boys I had known since kindergarten.

The first year at college, I was determined not to be shy any longer. I wanted to learn how to kiss with confidence and grace. I did.

In the spring, I went
home. I walked into the latest
hangout, and who do you
suppose I see sitting at the bar,
but my old kissing partner.
I walked over to his barstool
and tapped him on the shoulder.
Without hesitation, I took him in
my arms, dipped him back over
his stool, and kissed him with my
most assertive kiss. I sat him up,

looked at him victoriously, and said, "So there!"

He pointed to the lady next to him and said to me, "Mary Jane, I'd like you to meet my wife."

— *Mary Jane West-Delgado*
  Chicken Soup for the Teenage Soul

Life is either a
daring adventure
or nothing at all.

HELEN KELLER

Always
Return Your
Phone Calls

Angela knew that Charlotte, her best friend, was having a rough time. Charlotte was moody and depressed. She was withdrawn around everyone except for Angela. She instigated arguments with her mom and had violent confrontations with her sister. Most of all, Charlotte's bleak and desperate poetry worried Angela.

No one was on particularly good speaking terms with Charlotte that summer. For most of her friends, Charlotte had become too difficult. They had no interest in hanging out with someone who was so bleak and in so much pain. Their attempts to "be a friend" were met with angry accusations or depressed indifference.

Angela was the only one

who could reach her. Although she would have liked to have been outside, Angela spent most of her time inside with her troubled friend. Then a day came when Angela had to move. She was going just across town, but Charlotte would no longer be her neighbor, and they would be spending far less time together.

The first day in her new

neighborhood, out playing with her new neighbors, Angela wondered how Charlotte was doing. When she got home, shortly before twilight, her mother told her Charlotte had called.

Angela went to the phone to return the call. No answer. She left a message on Charlotte's machine. "Hi Charlotte, it's Angela. Call me back."

About half an hour later

Charlotte called. "Angela, I
have to tell you something.
When you called, I was in
the basement. I had a gun
to my head. I was about to kill
myself, but then I heard your
voice on the machine upstairs."

Angela collapsed into
her chair.

"When I heard your
voice I realized someone loves
me, and I am so lucky that it

is you. I'm going to get help, because I love you, too."

Charlotte hung up the phone. Angela went right over to Charlotte's house, and they sat on the porch swing and cried.

— *Anonymous*
  Chicken Soup for the Teenage Soul

When you give of yourself, you receive more than you give.

ANTOINE de SAINT EXUPÉRY

Growing

I'm leaving, Mother, hear me go!
Please wish me luck today.
I've grown my wings,
        I want to fly,
Seize my victories where
        they lie.
I'm going, Mom, but please
        don't cry—
Just let me find my way.
I want to see and touch
        and hear,
Though there are dangers,

there are fears.
I'll smile my smiles and dry
my tears—
Please let me speak my say.
I'm off to find my world,
my dreams,
Carve my niche, sew my seams,
Remember, as I sail my streams—
I'll love you, all the way.

— *Brooke Mueller*
Chicken Soup for the Teenage Soul

Don't bug me. Hug me!

— Bumper Sticker

The Secret of Happiness

There is a wonderful fable about a young orphan girl who had no family and no one to love her. One day, feeling exceptionally sad and lonely, she was walking through a meadow when she noticed a small butterfly caught unmercifully in a thornbush. The more the butterfly struggled to free itself, the deeper the thorns cut into its fragile body. The young orphan girl carefully released the butterfly from its captivity. Instead of flying away, the little butterfly changed into a beautiful fairy. The young girl rubbed her eyes in disbelief.

"For your wonderful kindness," the good fairy said to the girl, "I will grant you any wish you would like."

The little girl thought for

a moment and then replied,
"I want to be happy!"

The fairy said, "Very well,"
and leaned toward her and
whispered in her ear. Then the
good fairy vanished.

As the little girl grew up,
there was no one in the land as
happy as she. Everyone asked
her the secret of her happiness.
She would only smile and answer,

"The secret of my happiness is that I listened to a good fairy when I was a little girl."

When she was very old and on her deathbed, the neighbors all rallied around her, afraid that her fabulous secret of happiness would die with her. "Tell us, please," they begged. "Tell us what the good fairy said."

The lovely old woman simply smiled and said, "She told

me that everyone, no matter
how secure they seemed, no
matter how old or young, how
rich or poor, had need of me."

— *The Speaker's Sourcebook*
  Chicken Soup for the Teenage Soul

What Is Success?

To laugh often and much;
To win the respect of
intelligent people and the
affection of children;

To earn the appreciation of
honest critics and endure the
betrayal of false friends;
To appreciate beauty;
To find the best in others;

To leave the world a bit better, whether by a healthy child, a garden patch or a redeemed social condition;

To know even one life has breathed easier because you have lived;

This is to have succeeded.

— Ralph Waldo Emerson
  Chicken Soup for the Teenage Soul

Reach high, for stars lie hidden in your soul. Dream deep, for every dream precedes the goal.

PAMELA VAULL STARR

What's Wrong?

A newly trained teacher named Mary went to teach at a Navajo Indian reservation. Every day, she would ask five of the young Navajo students to go to the chalkboard and complete a simple math problem from their homework. They would stand there, silently, unwilling to complete the task. Mary couldn't figure it out. Nothing she had studied in her educational curriculum helped, and she certainly hadn't seen anything like it in her student-teaching days back in Phoenix.

What am I doing wrong? Could I have chosen five students who can't do the problem? Mary would wonder. No, it couldn't be that. Finally she asked the students what was wrong. And in their answer, she learned a surprising lesson from her young Indian

pupils about self-image and
a sense of self-worth.

It seemed that the
students respected each other's
individuality and knew that not
all of them were capable of
doing the problems. Even at
their early age, they understood
the senselessness of the win-lose
approach in the classroom. They
believed no one would win if any
students were shown up or

embarrassed at the chalkboard. So they refused to compete with each other in public.

Once she understood, Mary changed the system so that she could check each child's math problem individually, but not at any child's expense in front of his classmates. They all wanted to learn—but not at someone else's expense.

— *The Speaker's Sourcebook*
  Chicken Soup for the Teenage Soul